Original title:
Starlight Chill

Copyright © 2024 Swan Charm
All rights reserved.

Author: Kaido Väinamäe
ISBN HARDBACK: 978-9916-79-345-9
ISBN PAPERBACK: 978-9916-79-346-6
ISBN EBOOK: 978-9916-79-347-3

Chills from the Canopies Above

Whispers drift from branches tall,
Leaves that dance, shadows fall.
Cool air wraps like a shroud,
Nature sings, soft and loud.

Misty mornings, light so dim,
Fingers trace the forest's rim.
A rustle speaks of life unseen,
In green depths, the world is keen.

The twilight casts ethereal sights,
Stars ignite, painting the nights.
Chills run down the spine of trees,
In stillness, heartbeats tease.

As clouds drift, secrets too,
Moonlit paths we wander through.
Fey shadows play on velvet ground,
In this magic, peace is found.

Beneath the boughs, echoes soar,
Ancient tales of yore explore.
With each step, whispers fade,
In the woods, souls are laid.

Secrets of the Silent Universe

Vast expanse, a cosmic sea,
Stars align, whispers free.
Galaxies spin in graceful dance,
In the void, lost souls prance.

Nebulas bloom with colors bright,
Painting stories in the night.
Infinite mysteries lie in wait,
Time entwines fate's soft gait.

Planets drift in solemn grace,
Silent beings weave through space.
Echoes of the big bang remain,
In the silence, truths contain.

Light years stretch like a timeless thread,
Lost in thoughts of those long dead.
Cosmos cradles hopes and dreams,
In its vastness, nothing seems.

Through the dark, distant light gleams,
Unfathomable, the universe schemes.
In each star, a story spun,
In the silence, all is one.

Echoes of Night's Glow

In shadows deep, the whispers play,
Soft moonlight dances, guiding sway.
Through fields of dreams, the starlight beams,
Awakening hopes from silent schemes.

Each twinkle calls, a secret shared,
In the hush of night, all fears laid bare.
The world a canvas, painted bright,
With echoes sweet of love's pure light.

Lullabies in Universes Unraveled

Beneath the vast and endless skies,
Where galaxies spin, and stardust lies.
A lullaby hums, soft and low,
In dreams entwined, we gently flow.

The fabric of time, it twists and bends,
As cosmic stories weave and blend.
In every heartbeat, a tale is spun,
Of timeless love, our spirits won.

Night's Tapestry of Frost

Upon the ground, a silver lace,
A frozen quilt, nature's embrace.
The night's breath weaves a chilling sigh,
As stars above begin to cry.

Each flake a wish, a moment's grace,
In fleeting time, we find our place.
With crystal dreams, the world aglow,
A tapestry rich in night's soft flow.

Flickers of Forgotten Glories

In corners dark, where memories sleep,
Flickers of light, their secrets keep.
Echoes of laughter, shadows of pain,
In the heart's archive, they still remain.

Each moment captured, held so tight,
In whispers low, they seek the light.
A journey traced through time's embrace,
Flickers of glories we still retrace.

Stars Adrift in Silence

Stars glisten softly above,
Lost in the velvet night.
Whispers of dreams take flight,
Carried on wings of light.

Waves of the cosmos roll,
Patterns in silent dance.
Each twinkle tells a tale,
Of fate and chance.

In the vastness we seek,
Secrets in the dark.
Celestial voices speak,
Sparking the heart's spark.

Floating through cosmic waves,
Time drifts like a sigh.
Moments infinitely brave,
Underneath the sky.

Constellations align,
Guiding the voyage home.
In stillness, minds intertwine,
Where lonely souls roam.

The Quietude Between Hearts

In whispers soft and low,
Two souls find their grace.
Unspoken words flow,
In silence, they embrace.

Gentle glances share,
The stories left untold.
In every moment bare,
A warmth that never grows cold.

Like a soft summer breeze,
Their spirits intertwine.
In the space between,
Love's true light does shine.

A symphony of peace,
Composed in tender trust.
In their quietude,
Life reveals its must.

Beneath the stars above,
In the night's quiet hold.
Two hearts dance as one,
In silence, pure and bold.

Frosted Wishes on the Wind

Winter's breath, a gentle chill,
Blankets of white unfold.
Frosted wishes in stillness stir,
As dreams begin to mold.

Whispers of hope take flight,
On the soft, crisp air.
Glistening stars shine bright,
A moment so rare.

Branches draped in silver lace,
Nature's art displayed.
In this serene embrace,
All worries seem to fade.

As the day meets the night,
A hush falls over all.
Frosted wishes take their flight,
In the serene snowfall.

With each crunch underfoot,
Promises in the air.
A world wrapped in beauty,
In stillness, we share.

Beneath the Night's Caress

Moonlight spills on the ground,
Casting shadows so deep.
In quietude, hearts abound,
As the world starts to sleep.

Stars twinkle like secrets,
Carried on whispers of night.
In their tranquil bequest,
Lost in dreams, we take flight.

The breeze sings a soft tune,
As trees sway with grace.
Embraced by the night's moon,
In this still, sacred space.

Underneath the sky's cloak,
Promises find their way.
With every word unspoke,
We welcome the new day.

Beneath the night's sweet glow,
Life's magic comes alive.
In the silence we know,
Together we will thrive.

Celestial Embrace

Stars twinkle dimly above,
Cradled in an endless sky,
The moon shines with gentle love,
Whispers of night softly sigh.

In cosmic arms, we find our place,
Floating in this vast expanse,
Time slows down, a slow embrace,
A silent waltz, a mystic dance.

Nebulas swirl in hues of light,
Painting dreams upon the night,
Galaxies spin with grace profound,
In this cradle, peace is found.

Comets streak with tales untold,
Echoes of the past unfold,
With every pulse, the universe sings,
A harmony of cosmic things.

Together, we drift through the void,
Fearful hearts are safely buoyed,
Underneath the stars up high,
In celestial embrace, we lie.

Night's Whispering Touch

The shadows dance, a silent song,
Night's caress, tender and long,
Every breeze a soothing breath,
Carrying whispers from the depths.

Soft starlight weaves through the trees,
Filling the world with mysteries,
Moonbeams gather like secrets shared,
In the stillness, we feel prepared.

Cool night air wraps around us tight,
In this moment, all feels right,
Nature's lullaby fills the night,
As dreams take wing in soft moonlight.

Each rustle holds a gentle tale,
Echoes of love that never pale,
With every sigh, the night draws near,
In night's embrace, our hearts are clear.

Together, we breathe in the dark,
Finding in silence a hidden spark,
Night's whispering touch, deep and true,
Awakens a magic meant for two.

Beneath the Cosmic Veil

A tapestry of twinkling stars,
Woven through the quiet night,
Cosmic wonders, near and far,
Drawing hearts to their pure light.

Planets glide on paths so bold,
Stories written in their flight,
Beneath the veil, we find our gold,
In the starlit embrace of night.

Galaxies swirl in colors bright,
With secrets held in every hue,
Each pulse of light a spark of life,
A universe that feels so new.

Underneath this vast expanse,
We discover dreams yet to bloom,
In this cosmic, timeless dance,
We meet the infinite in the gloom.

Together, we gaze at the sky,
Finding solace in the unknown,
Beneath the veil, you and I,
In a universe we call our own.

Frigid Radiance

Frosty air glimmers at dawn,
Whispers of winter's icy breath,
Crystal branches, silver spawn,
Painting the world in quiet death.

The sun breaks through, a warming light,
Stirrings under a fragile shell,
Nature wakes from the long night,
In frigid radiance, all is well.

Each flake that falls a fleeting kiss,
Blanketing earth in purest white,
With every sparkle, there's a bliss,
As silence calms the morning light.

The chill embraces every breath,
In beauty found where cold does reign,
Yet warmth awaits, a promise kept,
As winter's grasp begins to wane.

Together, we wander, hand in hand,
Through landscapes dressed in glistening hue,
In this realm, enchantments stand,
Frigid radiance, blessed and true.

Celestial Chill

The night sky whispers cold,
Stars like diamonds unfold.
Moonlight drapes the world so still,
In this tranquil, cosmic thrill.

Winds carry tales from far away,
Echoes of night dance and sway.
Beneath the vast celestial dome,
Hearts find warmth, and spirits roam.

Frosted breath in chilling air,
Nature's heart, so pure, so rare.
Every breath a misty plume,
In the night's embrace, I bloom.

Eternity held in a glance,
In this quiet, cosmic dance.
Galaxies twirl, their secrets shared,
In silence, all creation stared.

A chill wraps round with gentle grace,
In the universe's vast embrace.
Stars shimmer like whispers made,
In the cool shadow where dreams cascaded.

Frozen Luminance

Icicles sparkle with pure light,
Casting prisms in the night.
A landscape draped in frosty white,
Nurtured by the moon's soft sight.

Glistening snow carpets the ground,
In each crystal, magic's found.
Whispers of winter weave a song,
As the night stretches, deep and long.

Trees stand tall in silvery glow,
Guardians of secrets, wise and slow.
Nature sleeps under starry shrouds,
Draped in tranquility's proud clouds.

A twinkle in the frosty air,
Promises of warmth somewhere.
Each moment, a gift of grace,
In this frozen, luminous space.

Frost-kissed dreams cradle the night,
A symphony of pure delight.
As silence wraps the world so tight,
Frozen luminance, a wondrous sight.

Glimmering Embrace

In the arms of the night, we dwell,
With the stars, we weave a spell.
Silvery beams like whispers glide,
In this realm where shadows reside.

The moon spills light across the land,
A glimmering touch, both soft and grand.
Each heartbeat echoes close and near,
Wrapped in warmth when you are here.

The night unfolds its velvet cloak,
In every sigh, an ember spoke.
With each glance, the cosmos twirls,
In the dance of starlit pearls.

Embrace the stillness, let it hold,
Stories of love quietly told.
Every moment a sparkling trace,
In the arms of a glimmering embrace.

Softly the cosmos twinkles bright,
Illuminating our shared flight.
Together we find, without a care,
In infinite love, a timeless air.

Stars in the Silence

Amidst the quiet, stars align,
In the dark, they brightly shine.
Each point of light, a distant tale,
In the silence, their whispers hail.

Veils of night wrap around our hearts,
As we search for worlds that part.
Lost in dreams, we softly sway,
In starlit paths, we find our way.

The cosmos breathes a gentle sigh,
Echoing the moments that fly.
In the stillness, hope ignites,
Guiding us through endless nights.

Every twinkle holds a prayer,
An invitation spun with care.
Together, in the hush, we sing,
The beauty only silence brings.

Stars in the silence paint the sky,
In this canvas, we dare to fly.
A universe rich with light and grace,
In the stillness, we find our place.

Crystal Dreams Against the Unseen

Beneath the stars of whispered light,
A dance of shadows takes its flight.
Fragments of hope in twilight's glean,
Shimmers of magic, softly unseen.

Echoes of laughter, soft and bright,
In the crystal dreams that tease the night.
Each flicker holds a promise dear,
Resonating softly, drawing near.

Through the mist where secrets play,
Wisps of joy drift far away.
Captured in glass, reflections gleam,
Life unfolds in fractured dream.

A journey woven through the air,
With crystalline paths, we learn to dare.
Hearts entwined in shimmering threads,
A tapestry where wonder spreads.

So tread lightly, where magic blends,
Among the dreams where journey bends.
In the unseen, let spirits soar,
For crystal dreams unlock the door.

Translucent Tranquility

In the stillness of the gentle night,
Moonlight dances, pure and bright.
Soft hymns of air breathe life anew,
Translucent whispers call to you.

Gentle ripples on a silver lake,
Where silence cradles each small break.
A fragile peace that softly sings,
Lifting spirits on delicate wings.

Through the fog, a soft embrace,
Caresses time, revealing grace.
Calm reflections in a world so vast,
Moments cherished, shadows cast.

Bright horizons, soothing glow,
In tranquil seas, the heart can flow.
Let worries fade, like twilight mist,
Find solace where the soul persists.

For in the quiet, heartbeats bloom,
In translucent light, dispelling gloom.
We walk the paths of moonlit streams,
And find ourselves in tranquil dreams.

Harmonies of the Glistening Dark

Night's embrace, with secrets shared,
Stars ignite, as dreams are bared.
A symphony in shadows spun,
Harmonies of dark, begun.

Beneath the veil of velvet skies,
Whispers echo, soft replies.
Each note a glimmer, shining bright,
Dancing gently in the night.

In the stillness, magic stirs,
Awakening dreams, the heart concurs.
The spell of night, both fierce and fair,
Threads of harmony weave through air.

Soundless songs on winter's breath,
Celebrate life, defy the death.
With every pulse, the dark ignites,
Harmonies bright in starry heights.

So listen closely to the sound,
Of glistening dark where dreams abound.
In shadows deep, find inner light,
As harmonies guide us through the night.

The Frosty Veil of Midnight

In winter's grip, the world lays still,
A frosty veil, the night's own thrill.
Moonbeams dance on blanket white,
Cloaking secrets wrapped in night.

Crystals gleam on every tree,
Nature's art, wild and free.
Whispers of chill in moonlit air,
Painting visions beyond compare.

Silent echoes of frost-kissed dreams,
Flowing softly like silver streams.
In the hour when shadows creep,
Midnight's magic, secrets keep.

Each breath a cloud, in silence flows,
A world adorned, the beauty grows.
Caught in wonder's gentle snare,
Where time pauses, free from care.

So under the frost, let spirits dance,
In the magic of a moonlit trance.
For in the stillness of the night,
The frosty veil reveals the light.

The Cosmic Breeze

In the night sky so vast,
Whispers of stars sing sweet,
Carrying dreams on the wings,
Through galaxies they fleet.

Celestial winds do play,
Caressing worlds anew,
Lifting hearts to the rhythm,
Of the cosmos' soft hue.

Nebulas swirl in delight,
Painting tales in the dark,
Each twinkle a delicate spark,
Creating a beautiful sight.

Dancing comets pass by,
Writing wishes in trails,
Beneath the watchful moon,
As the universe exhales.

In this cosmic embrace,
Feel the infinite call,
A connection so deep,
Binding us one and all.

Winter's Star Dance

Snowflakes twirl from the sky,
A waltz of frosty cheer,
Underneath the pale stars,
Whispers of winter near.

Trees dressed in shimmering white,
Glow softly in the night,
Crystals catch the moonlight,
Creating pure delight.

Footsteps crunch on the ground,
Echoes of laughter ring,
As winter's magic unfolds,
In the chill, joy takes wing.

Candles flicker with warmth,
As fires crackle bright,
Gathering close around,
In the embrace of night.

Time stands still in this scene,
As the world holds its breath,
In the dance of snowflakes,
Life's beauty knows no death.

Glistening Tranquility

Soft whispers of the stream,
Bathe the twilight in grace,
Nature's quiet embrace,
In the warmth of a dream.

Leaves rustle gently by,
As the sun dips below,
Painting skies with a glow,
In the evening's lullaby.

Stillness reigns in the air,
Moonlight shimmers on water,
A calming flow to the soul,
In peace, hearts grow lighter.

Crickets serenade night,
Under a tapestry of stars,
Each note, a sweet caress,
Healing all of our scars.

In this moment we find,
The world's beauty revealed,
A glistening tranquility,
In nature's arms, we're healed.

Twilight's Breath

As day whispers goodbye,
Colors bleed into night,
A canvas of crimson
And soft shades of twilight.

Birds settle in the trees,
Songs fade into sweet hush,
Under a blanket of stars,
The evening begins to blush.

Cool breezes gently sweep,
Carrying scents of the earth,
Mingling with twilight's breath,
In silence, we find worth.

Shadows dance as they play,
Beneath the crescent moon,
Whispers of secrets hold,
In the night's soft cocoon.

In this serene embrace,
Time feels like it's suspended,
Wrapped in twilight's love,
Where every moment is splendid.

Spectrum of the Silent Eve

The sky drapes soft in hues of gray,
Where whispers dance and shadows play.
Each color fades, a fleeting sigh,
As day retreats, and night draws nigh.

Beneath the trees, the crickets hum,
Echoing tales of what's to come.
Stars awaken in the velvet dark,
While glowing embers leave their mark.

A tender breeze weaves through the leaves,
In every gust, a secret weaves.
The world slows down, a tranquil breath,
Embracing stillness, over death.

Moonlight spills on the dewy grass,
Where time stands still, as moments pass.
In twilight's hold, the stillness thrives,
Embracing dreams, where silence strives.

So let us linger, lost in time,
In silence, we shall feel the rhyme.
For in the quiet, beauty lives,
A spectrum lost, yet still it gives.

Luminescence in the Hush

In twilight's glow, the world unwinds,
Where gentle shadows wrap what shines.
A whisper soft, the night unfolds,
With stories told in glimmers bold.

The stars ignite, a distant choir,
Each spark a dream, a burning fire.
They flicker dreams in velvet skies,
While silent wishes slowly rise.

Amidst the calm, the heartbeats swell,
In every pause, a tale to tell.
The night enfolds with tender grace,
A luminescence in space's embrace.

Through every hush, the moments gleam,
A fragile thread of light and dream.
As darkness weaves its mystic song,
In silence deep, where souls belong.

So let us drift in quiet bliss,
In this soft glow, a timeless kiss.
For in the hush, the world awakes,
Where every heart in silence aches.

Memory of an Icy Horizon

A canvas white, where dreams reside,
In frozen breath, the world confides.
The horizon stretches, crisp and clear,
Reflecting hopes, both far and near.

Amidst the chill, the whispers freeze,
Each frozen flake, a thought that flees.
The silence wraps the earth so tight,
In memory's grasp, the pale moonlight.

Footprints lie where no one goes,
A journey traced in the winter's prose.
The echo of laughter lingers on,
In icy breaths, a love that's gone.

When twilight falls, the colors blend,
As daylight fades, and shadows mend.
Within this realm of time's embrace,
The past persists in cold's sharp face.

So let us walk in layers bright,
Through shimmering dreams in frosted light.
For in this icy world we find,
A memory etched, forever blind.

The Frozen Calm of Midnight

At midnight's gate, the world lies still,
In quiet grace, the night fulfills.
A breath of frost on window panes,
Where dreams take flight in silver chains.

The moon a guardian high and bright,
Watches over the shrouded night.
Each star a friend in velvet space,
As shadows dance with ghostly grace.

In solitude, the whispers creep,
The secrets that the dark can keep.
And time, it drips like melting ice,
In frozen calm, a soft suffice.

With every heartbeat, silence swells,
While nature sings its ancient spells.
A lullaby of peace and calm,
In midnight's arms, we find the balm.

So take a breath and close your eyes,
For in the void, the spirit flies.
Embrace the still, the world asleep,
In frozen calm, our souls shall leap.

Ethereal Frigidness

In shadows cast by winter's breath,
The stars emerge, a silent death.
A whisper cold, the night does keep,
While icy winds through branches creep.

Beneath a sky of diamond light,
The world is wrapped in silver white.
A frozen dance of twinkling grace,
In nature's still and quiet space.

The trees adorned with crystal lace,
Hold secrets of a tranquil place.
Each flake a story, unique, untold,
A fleeting moment, pure and bold.

As whispers fade into the dark,
The chill ignites a frozen spark.
In every breath, the world exhales,
An ethereal tone, where stillness prevails.

Embrace the cold, embrace the night,
For in this frigidness, there's light.
In silence deep, life stirs and waves,
Ethereal whispers in hidden caves.

Cosmic Hush

In the quiet of the vast unknown,
Where stars are seeds, gently sown.
A breath of time, a moment's pause,
In cosmic hush, the universe draws.

The galaxies swirl in graceful dance,
With every glance, we find our chance.
To lose ourselves in endless flight,
Under the cloak of the velvet night.

Orbs of light that flicker, gleam,
Awaken distant, dreamy dreams.
A silent song from skies above,
Resounding echoes of endless love.

In the stillness, a heartbeat found,
Boundless whispers that swirl around.
The secrets of space, tenderly weave,
In this hush, the cosmos believe.

Drifting through the fabric of night,
Find solace in the stars' soft light.
In cosmic hush, let worries cease,
And find within a fleeting peace.

Veins of Ice

Through winters harsh, the rivers freeze,
With veins of ice, they twist with ease.
Nature's hand forms crystal streams,
Reflecting frost of hollow dreams.

The surface glints, like glass so clear,
A chilling magic draws us near.
Each line, a story carved by cold,
Of whispered tales from ages old.

Where silence reigns in frozen lands,
And beauty lies in nature's hands.
These veins of ice, a path of grace,
Hold mysteries in their cool embrace.

As shadows dance on glistening trails,
The heart of winter softly pales.
In each frozen breath, life lies close,
Veins of ice, where quiet flows.

A moment caught in crystal time,
A frozen world, a quiet rhyme.
Within the chill, warmth says goodbye,
And dreams unfold beneath the sky.

Dreaming Under the Moon

In silver glow, the soft light beams,
As night unfolds our hidden dreams.
The world transformed, a gentle view,
Where whispers drift and shadows, too.

Underneath this watchful eye,
We weave our hopes, and sighs comply.
With every pulse of twilight's kiss,
We chase the stars, embrace the bliss.

The moonlight dances on tranquil lakes,
In every wave, a memory wakes.
With silvered paths that guide our way,
Through veils of night, the heart will play.

In dreaming hours, our souls take flight,
In twilight magic, all feels right.
Each heartbeat syncs with time's refrain,
Under the moon, our fears remain.

So let us dream where echoes sigh,
With every wish that sails on high.
In moonlit realms, our spirits meet,
Where night and dreams in silence greet.

Chilled Radiance

Moonlight bathes the quiet ground,
Whispers peace in every sound.
Shadows dance upon the trees,
Carried softly by the breeze.

Frosty breath on winter's night,
Sparkles twinkling, pure delight.
Nature sleeps in shimmering grace,
As stars adorn the vast space.

Stillness reigns in silver hue,
Hearts find solace, calm and true.
Every moment, soft and bright,
Wrapped in chilled, enchanting light.

Underneath the endless sky,
Dreams take flight, they soar and fly.
In this time of frosted beams,
Life unfolds in quiet dreams.

Chilled radiance, softly poured,
A gentle gift, forever stored.
Beneath the night, all feels right,
In the glow of soft moonlight.

Starlit Solitude

In the silence, stars appear,
Whispers of the night so clear.
Alone beneath the open dome,
Finding peace, a sweetened home.

Each twinkle tells a tale long spun,
Of journeys taken, battles won.
Wrapped in darkness, yet so bright,
Solitude feels warm tonight.

Winds of change now softly sigh,
Floating thoughts like clouds nearby.
Crystal glimmers on the lake,
Mirror worlds where dreams can wake.

Time unravels, slow and free,
In this sacred space, just me.
Stars bear witness to my dreams,
Guiding journeys, like moonbeams.

Starlit paths unfold ahead,
Every step, by courage led.
In the quiet night's embrace,
I find strength, a sacred place.

Glittering Nightscape

Canvas black with dots of light,
Drawing eyes to wondrous sight.
Mountains high and valleys low,
Embrace the night's majestic glow.

Crickets sing a gentle tune,
While the silver slips from moon.
Trees adorned in shadows cast,
Stories linger from the past.

Each breath taken, crisp and clear,
Nature whispers, drawing near.
In the stillness, dreams ignite,
Painting life in shades of night.

Stars align in perfect grace,
Mapping out this timeless space.
With every twinkle, secrets spill,
Awakening a restless will.

Glittering jewels in the sky,
Threads of fate that never die.
In the nightscape, wild and free,
I discover the heart of me.

Frosty Night's Kiss

When the world is dressed in white,
Crisp and sharp, the stars are bright.
Every breath a cloud of mist,
Marking moments not to miss.

Frozen rivers softly gleam,
Cerulean in the moon's beam.
Footsteps crunch on snowy ground,
In this stillness, peace is found.

Night unfolds, a velvet cloak,
Wrapped in whispers, dreams evoke.
Frosty air awakens souls,
Comfort found in gentle roles.

Every flake a work of art,
Graceful dance, and nature's heart.
Softly falls, a quiet bliss,
Captured in a frosty kiss.

Through the night, the magic flows,
In the stillness, wonder grows.
Frosty night, your elegance,
Leaves a lasting resonance.

Shimmering Cold

Ice crystals dance in the silver night,
Whispers of frost in the pale moonlight.
Bitter winds weave through silent trees,
Nature's breath carries a frosty tease.

Stars twinkle like diamonds in darkened skies,
Melodies of winter, soft lullabies.
Footprints mark a path in the fresh, white snow,
Echoes of stillness where cold breezes blow.

The world wears a gown of glistening white,
A shivering hush cloaked in soft twilight.
Frozen branches stretch in a graceful arc,
Revealing secrets hidden in the dark.

Under this chill, the earth takes a pause,
Wrapped in a blanket, it breathes without cause.
Time moves slowly, as moments unfold,
Cradled in beauty, the shimmering cold.

In the quiet realm where silence reigns,
Fleeting thoughts dance through winter's chains.
Each breath a cloud, each heart a beat,
Bound by the frost, in time we meet.

Beneath the Cosmic Veil

In the depths of night where shadows play,
Stars twinkle softly, guiding the way.
Secrets of ages drift through the dark,
Whispers of ancients, a celestial spark.

Galaxies swirl in a cosmic dance,
Infinite wonders invite a glance.
Planets like gems in the velvet sea,
Lost in the fabric of destiny.

Nebulas blossom in vibrant hues,
Painting the skies with chromatic views.
Constellations weave tales of the past,
Stories of lovers, and dreams that last.

Beneath this vast and eternal dome,
We search for meaning, we seek a home.
In the silence, our souls intertwine,
Bound by the stardust, our fates align.

As we gaze upward with hopes untold,
The night unfolds with its mysteries bold.
Beneath the cosmic veil, we reside,
Cradled in wonders, where dreams abide.

Luminescent Tranquility

Soft light dances on the lake's smooth face,
Ripples shimmer, time slows its pace.
Moonbeams touch the water's gentle sway,
A hush blankets night, where shadows play.

In the stillness, a heart finds peace,
Moments suspended, all worries cease.
Whispers of nature soothe the weary mind,
In this embrace, solace we find.

Trees stand tall, guardians of the night,
Glowing softly, wrapped in silver light.
Stars gaze down, with secrets to share,
In this tranquil place, we breathe the air.

Each breath a rhythm, a calming song,
Harmony reigns, where souls belong.
Lost in the beauty of the quiet glow,
Kindness of night, in this moment, we flow.

Luminescent whispers of gentle dreams,
Floating on currents, like delicate streams.
In this realm of peace, our spirits fly,
Together we wander, beneath the sky.

Hushed Nocturne

The night unfolds, a velvet embrace,
Moonlight spills softly, filling the space.
Stars shimmer gently, a muted tune,
Hushed nocturne plays to the heart of June.

Amidst the shadows, secrets reside,
In whispered breezes, dreams confide.
Soft rustling leaves, a serenade sweet,
Nature's own rhythm, a heartbeat's repeat.

Distant echoes of a lullaby sung,
Filling the silence where memories hung.
Time drifts slowly, wrapped in a sigh,
The world bathed in peace, as night whispers by.

Beneath the canopy, wrapped in the dark,
Silent wishes ignite like a spark.
Moments cascade like dew on a rose,
In this hush, the soul truly knows.

As dawn approaches, the softness will wane,
Yet in this stillness, forever remain.
A hushed nocturne, a timeless refrain,
Echoes of night where dreams will sustain.

Bedtime Stories from the Cosmos

In skies where dreams take flight,
The moon whispers soft goodnight,
Stars twinkle in gentle sway,
Guiding the lost on their way.

Galaxies spin tales untold,
Of heroes brave and hearts bold,
Nebulas cradle hopes anew,
In the vastness, we're never through.

Comets race with fiery tails,
Carrying wishes on their trails,
Each twinkle a promise made,
In the silence, dreams aren't laid.

Cosmic lullabies hum sweet,
As stardust blankets our feet,
Listen, the universe sings,
To the rhythm of endless springs.

So close your eyes and drift afar,
In this realm where dreams are star,
Find solace in the night's embrace,
Bedtime stories leave no trace.

A Dance Beneath the Frozen Stars

In the quiet of winter's grace,
A gentle frost begins to lace,
Footprints cradle the whispering snow,
As night falls, the cold winds blow.

Waltzing shadows under the glow,
Of distant stars that softly show,
A choreography in the night,
Where hearts beat in pure delight.

Each twirl a tale of joy and pain,
The rhythm of love, an endless chain,
In the deep silence, echoes of dreams,
Mingle with the moonbeam's gleams.

Icicles hang like glistening chimes,
Playing the song of ancient times,
A melody weaves through the air,
Binding the earth with starry flair.

So dance beneath the frozen stars,
Let go of worries, heal your scars,
In the stillness, find your part,
As winter cradles your beating heart.

Elysian Twilight Hues

When dusk descends in hues so bright,
The sky transforms with fading light,
Brushstrokes of lavender and gold,
Stories of the day unfold.

Clouds drift like whispers of dreams,
Woven with sunlight's gentle beams,
The horizon blushes, bathed in fire,
With every second, hearts aspire.

Twilight dances, coy and shy,
As a tapestry of stars draws nigh,
Each twinkle a wish, a hope regained,
In this quiet, bliss unchained.

The world basks in serene embrace,
Time slows down, finding its place,
Nature sighs in colors true,
In deepening night, we're reborn anew.

So linger long in twilight's grace,
Let your soul find its sacred space,
In elysian hues, dreams ignite,
Painted gently by fading light.

Echoing the Universe's Breath

In silence deep, the cosmos breathes,
Each pulse a secret, softly weaves,
Galaxies hum a timeless tune,
A symphony beneath the moon.

Stars blink in rhythm, dance of fate,
Echoes of whispers, we contemplate,
Waves of existence crash and flow,
In the vastness, all life grows.

Nebulas cloak the dark unknown,
In their embrace, new worlds are sown,
Every heartbeat a spark divine,
Merging with the grand design.

The universe speaks in endless grace,
In every void, we find our place,
Space unfolds in colors bold,
A tapestry of truths untold.

So breathe with the stars, in sync with time,
Let the rhythm awaken your rhyme,
For in this dance of life's sweet thread,
We are the echoes of all that's said.

Luminous Dreams in the Dark

In shadows deep, where whispers play,
The stars awake and lead the way.
A glimmer soft, a spark so bright,
Guiding hearts through the endless night.

In silent vows, our wishes soar,
Embracing hope, forevermore.
Through tangled paths, our spirits chase,
The beauty found in boundless space.

When midnight calls, we drift and weave,
In vibrant hues, we dare believe.
Each dream a thread, a story spun,
Illuminated by the moon and sun.

With every breath, the night unfolds,
A tapestry of tales retold.
In luminous dreams, we find our grace,
A gentle light in this vast embrace.

Together, we will chase the dawn,
Where hopes are born, and fears are gone.
In every pulse, our souls align,
In luminous dreams, forever shine.

Ethereal Glow

A flicker soft, a gentle beam,
In twilight's hush, we start to dream.
With every pulse, the world takes flight,
An ethereal glow ignites the night.

Through golden fields, the whispers flow,
A dance of light, an ageless show.
The essence of the stars above,
Wraps our hearts in tender love.

As dusk descends, the shadows creep,
Yet in our souls, the embers keep.
For in this place, the magic swells,
An ethereal glow, our spirit tells.

In quiet moments, silence speaks,
A harmony the heart so seeks.
We chase the glow, we seize the hour,
In every breath, we find our power.

Together we will light the sky,
With dreams that shimmer, spirits fly.
In sacred moments, let love show,
In every heartbeat, an ethereal glow.

Frost-kissed Memories

Amidst the chill of winter's breath,
Lies warmth that conquers quiet death.
With every flake that falls and sways,
Frost-kissed memories weave their ways.

In whispered winds, old tales unfold,
Of love and laughter, bright and bold.
Each crystal spark, a story's trace,
In frosted time, we find our place.

Beneath the moon's soft silver sheen,
The past awakens, calm yet keen.
From icy veils, hearts dance in glee,
Embracing all that's meant to be.

As snowflakes twirl, we dream anew,
In crystalline, the past shines through.
With every breath, the chill ignites,
Frost-kissed memories, endless nights.

Let's gather 'round the fire's light,
To share our tales beneath the night.
In the warmth of hearts, we find our way,
Frost-kissed memories, here to stay.

Celestial Serenade

In twilight's arms, the stars align,
A celestial serenade divine.
With melodies that softly hum,
The cosmos sings, the night becomes.

Glimmers bright, in hues so pure,
Whispers of dreams, forever sure.
The universe in symphony flows,
In endless dance, our spirit knows.

As constellations weave their tales,
The heart catches, and wonder sails.
Through cosmic winds, we gently glide,
In celestial serenades, we abide.

Each note a bridge from here to there,
A timeless bond, a love to share.
In the stillness, our spirits soar,
In celestial dreams, forevermore.

Together, we will light the sky,
Awake the wonder, let hopes fly.
In harmony, our souls cascade,
In cosmic peace, a serenade.

Nebula's Embrace

In the depths of night sky's quilt,
Stars shimmer like dreams unbuilt.
Galaxies spin in silent grace,
Wrapped in the nebula's embrace.

Colors dance in cosmic twirl,
Mysteries of the universe whirl.
Where light and shadow interlace,
Lost in the nebula's embrace.

Whispers echo through the void,
In this realm, the heart's destroyed.
Yet hope glimmers in this space,
Cradled by the nebula's embrace.

Each moment feels like endless flight,
Certain and unsure, wrong and right.
In every pulse, we find our place,
Eternal in the nebula's embrace.

When the dawn breaks, colors blend,
From this journey, we shall bend.
Forever seeking, lost in chase,
Forever held in nebula's embrace.

Whispering Chill

The night air carries secrets old,
In whispered tones, the chill unfolds.
Every breath a frosty sigh,
As shadows stretch beneath the sky.

Leaves murmur tales of fleeting days,
In the quiet, their voices raise.
Beneath the moon's soft, silvered eye,
Time pauses, as moments fly.

Frost-kissed dreams and silent trails,
Life's essence wrapped in winter's veils.
With each heartbeat, the night will fill,
Embracing all in whispering chill.

Stars peek through the velvet dark,
Guiding dreams like a distant spark.
In the stillness, echoes thrill,
Held tight in the whispering chill.

As the dawn breaks, the chill will fade,
Yet memories linger, softly laid.
A tender touch, a peaceful thrill,
Forever felt in whispering chill.

Celestial Cascade

Waterfalls of stardust fall,
In silent grace, they heed the call.
Rivers of light in cosmic dance,
Drawing eyes with a timeless glance.

Each droplet holds a story bright,
Of endless realms woven in night.
Caught in a wondrous, swirling trance,
Flowing through the celestial cascade.

Where dreams and wishes intertwine,
A canvas vast, a secret sign.
In this journey, we chance to prance,
Lost in the celestial cascade.

Waves of color, soft and bold,
Through the darkness, the light unfolds.
Every heartbeat, a wild chance,
Swaying in the celestial cascade.

Beneath the vast, eternal dome,
We find our place, we call it home.
In this cosmic rhythm, we advance,
Forever swept in celestial cascade.

Midnight's Caress

Midnight blooms with a gentle sigh,
As shadows stretch, and dreams amplify.
Stars above in quiet dance,
Every heartbeat, a fleeting chance.

Cool winds whisper through the trees,
Carrying secrets on the breeze.
Wrapped in the night's soft embrace,
We lose ourselves in midnight's caress.

Moments linger, then drift away,
In the stillness, we choose to stay.
A world revealed in night's embrace,
Forever blessed by midnight's caress.

The moonlight casts enchanting spells,
Where every thought and feeling dwells.
In the silence, we find our grace,
Touched by the magic of midnight's caress.

As dawn approaches, dreams may fade,
Yet echoes linger, softly laid.
In every sigh, we sense its trace,
Carried gently by midnight's caress.

Glacial Harmony

In the stillness of ice-bound streams,
A whispering breeze holds quiet dreams.
Gentle crystals dance in a fleeting light,
Nature's breath glows in the heart of night.

Beneath the skies so vast, so clear,
Each snowflake falls, both far and near.
Frozen melodies weave through the air,
Echoes of time without a care.

Mountains stand tall, guardians of peace,
Cradling whispers that never cease.
In the realm where the cold winds play,
Harmony lingers, night and day.

Stars arise in the velvet dome,
Lonely, they flicker, calling us home.
Each twinkling light tells a story old,
Of glacial wonders, bright and bold.

As dawn awakes with tender grace,
The world transforms, a soft embrace.
In the warmth of the sun's warming rays,
Glacial harmony bids us stay.

Silvered Dreams

A shimmer glows on the edge of night,
Where silver whispers weave pure delight.
Floating softly on pillows of air,
Dreams take flight without a care.

The moonlight bathes the world in grace,
Painting shadows upon the space.
Gentle echoes of laughter play,
In the realm where dreams sway.

Silvery streams of thoughts cascade,
In the quiet dark, our fears fade.
The glow of memories wrap us tight,
Guiding us through the tranquil night.

Stars adorn the deep azure dome,
In their light, we wander home.
Each silver thread pulls the heart near,
In dreams, we find what we hold dear.

Awake to find the dawn's embrace,
But silver dreams still linger in space.
A tapestry of night twirls bright,
Whispering secrets in morning's light.

Enveloping Darkness

In shadows deep, the silence sighs,
Where mystery dwells beneath dark skies.
Veils of night draw close and tight,
Embracing all in gentle fright.

Whispers linger, secrets spun,
In the stillness, the dark is fun.
Each heartbeat echoes, soft and low,
Guiding us through the night's shadow.

Stars appear, like diamonds born,
Adorning dark with light reborn.
Yet in the depths of somber hues,
Life's hidden wonders softly muse.

The moon, a sentinel aglow,
Watches as old tales overflow.
In the backdrop of blackened streams,
Truths are found in timeless dreams.

As night envelopes, fears take flight,
In darkness lies a strange delight.
For in the hush, we often see,
The beauty that sets our spirits free.

Moonbeam Delight

When the moon spills light on the ground,
A silver glow whispers all around.
Dancing shadows creep and play,
In the magic of the moonlit sway.

Glowing beams of softest gold,
Crafting dreams that remain untold.
Where laughter lands on starlit grass,
Moments captured as hours pass.

Waves of twilight wash over the earth,
Igniting the night with a joyous mirth.
Each shimmer bright, a story to tell,
Drawing hearts in its spell.

Beneath the sky, so wide and bright,
We twirl like dancers in the soft light.
With every beat, our spirits ignite,
In the glimmer of moonbeam delight.

As dawn approaches, colors blend,
But moonbeam memories never end.
In the quiet, a promise laid,
Of moments cherished, never to fade.

Starlit Murmurs

In the night, whispers flow,
Silver beams, soft and low.
Dancing dreams on velvet skies,
Echoing where the silence lies.

Moonlit paths, a gentle guide,
Secrets held where shadows bide.
Awakening the heart's delight,
Beneath the hush of starlit light.

Winds carry tales of old,
Stories hidden, softly told.
Boundless eyes that seek to see,
The endless waltz of memory.

Glimmers weave in cosmic thread,
Where every thought and hope is bred.
A tapestry spun in the night,
Luminous, pure, a precious sight.

In the calm, let worries cease,
Wrapped in tranquil, sweet release.
As starlit murmurs softly call,
In this moment, we are all.

A Symphony in the Cold

Chill winds play a haunting tune,
Whispers echo 'neath the moon.
Frost and shadow intertwine,
Crafting magic, pure, divine.

Each flake falls like note so clear,
Melodies for hearts to hear.
Frozen symphonies arise,
Underneath the starry skies.

Crystalline air, fresh and bright,
Lends its voice to the night.
Softly it hums, quietly bold,
Tales of warmth in winter's cold.

Nature's orchestra unfolds,
In its grasp, the world beholds.
From silence grows a vibrant sound,
In this chill, love can be found.

As we listen, hearts engage,
In this symphony, we wage.
A dance of souls, both young and old,
In the harmony of the cold.

Nebula's Tender Touch

In shadows deep, colors bloom,
Whispers cradle the endless gloom.
Stars are born in swirling grace,
Nebula's soft, embracing space.

Painted skies, a cosmic dream,
Flowing gently like a stream.
Gentle breaths of starlit light,
Weaving magic through the night.

Each hue sings a secrets hymn,
Of worlds lost, now found in whim.
Radiant waves of light unfold,
Stories of the brave and bold.

Canvas vast, with stars as brush,
In this quiet, peaceful hush.
Touched by grace, we drift and sway,
Nebula's love lights the way.

Embrace the calm, let spirits rise,
In the tender, cosmic skies.
Where dreams are born, and time stands still,
With nebula's touch, we feel.

Embrace of the Cosmic Chill

Awake beneath a cosmic shroud,
Wrapped in night, serene and proud.
Whispers echo, soft and clear,
In the still, the stars draw near.

Embraced by winter's freezing breath,
We find solace in the depth.
Chilled air sparks a fire within,
Where dreams take flight, let life begin.

Galaxies spin in rhythmic grace,
Painting silence in this space.
Each twinkle holds a secret sigh,
As the cosmos whispers why.

In this chill, a warmth ignites,
Creating comfort in the nights.
Underneath this azure dome,
Each heartbeat finds its way back home.

So let the stars our hearts fulfill,
In their glow, we find our will.
A cosmic dance in tranquil sway,
In the chill, we find our way.

Chasing Celestial Breezes

In twilight's grasp, we float so free,
With stars that dance, they tease the sea.
A gentle touch upon our skin,
We chase the winds where dreams begin.

Among the clouds, our laughter rings,
A symphony of whispered things.
The moonlight guides our eager flight,
As constellations burn so bright.

Through cosmic streams, we sail and gleam,
Caught in this ever-daring dream.
The universe calls, a siren song,
With every breath, we all belong.

Past distant worlds, where wonders lie,
We glide beneath the endless sky.
Our hearts align with starlit grace,
In chasing breezes, we find our place.

So let us soar and never cease,
In celestial winds, we find our peace.
With galaxies swirling in our gaze,
We'll dance forever through the haze.

Frozen Light of the Universe

Beneath a veil of glittering night,
The cosmos glows with frozen light.
Each star a gem, so distant, rare,
Illuminates the still, cold air.

In silence deep, the galaxies spin,
A tapestry that holds within.
The whispers of time, a spark divine,
In frozen shrouds, our dreams entwine.

We stand in awe, our hearts ablaze,
Caught in the wonder, lost in the gaze.
Light years away, yet so close, it seems,
The universe cradles our wildest dreams.

Frosted worlds, where shadows creep,
In starlit secrets, the silence we keep.
Each beat of time, a tender glow,
In hushed embraces, we ebb and flow.

Together we wander, hand in hand,
Through frozen realms, vast expanses grand.
A dance of light, both calm and immense,
In the frozen light, we find our sense.

Whispers of the Frosty Abyss

In the depths where shadows wail,
The frost holds secrets in its veil.
Whispers echo, soft and low,
From ancient depths, where cold winds blow.

A chilling breath, a haunting song,
In the abyss, we drift along.
With every turn, the past unveils,
In frosty tales, our courage trails.

Embrace the chill, let it surround,
In icy realms, our fears unbound.
The whispers guide like distant stars,
As we unravel our hidden scars.

Through frosted dreams, our spirits rise,
We weave our fate in endless skies.
In the abyss, the truth reveals,
Heartfelt whispers the silence heals.

So fear not the depths that hold the night,
For in the frost, there shines a light.
Together we brave the cold's embrace,
In whispers soft, we find our grace.

Gentle Radiance Unfurled

As daybreak kisses the slumbering earth,
A gentle glow, a time of rebirth.
With every dawn, the colors bloom,
A soft embrace dispels the gloom.

Golden rays dance on dew-kissed grass,
In nature's arms, where moments pass.
The world awakens with tender sighs,
A symphony as the daylight flies.

The whispering winds carry dreams anew,
And every heartbeat draws us through.
With open hearts, we greet the morn,
In gentle radiance, we are reborn.

Through valleys wide and mountains tall,
The light cascades, unifying all.
Wrapped in warmth, we find our way,
In golden hues that chase the gray.

So let us bask in this radiant glow,
Together, where the wildflowers grow.
In every beam, a story swirls,
As nature whispers, our hearts unfurl.

Celestial Whispers

In the hush of night, stars gleam bright,
Whispers of dreams take flight,
Softly the cosmos sings,
Of hopes and hidden things.

Galaxies dance in heavenly swirl,
Fleeting moments unfurl,
Each twinkle a tale to tell,
In this celestial spell.

The moon casts a silver glow,
Guiding the wanderers below,
With every breath, we share,
The secrets hanging in the air.

Nebulae in vibrant hues,
Painting the night with muses,
Echoes of life in the void,
In the darkness, we find joy.

Eternal silence speaks so loud,
Connecting every heart and crowd,
In these celestial whispers,
We gather, skimming the blisters.

Frosted Dreams

In the chill of night, crystals gleam,
Nature's canvas, a tranquil dream,
Snowflakes twirl, softly they fall,
Whispering secrets to one and all.

The world dressed in a frosty lace,
Hiding warmth in a gentle embrace,
Underneath the winter's glow,
Awakens hope in every flake's flow.

Frozen branches, adorned like stars,
Beneath the moon, they dance from afar,
Each breath a cloud, rising with ease,
In the stillness, hearts find peace.

A soft hush blankets the earth,
Nurturing dreams and rebirth,
In this winter wonderland,
We grasp the magic, hand in hand.

Frosted dreams linger and sway,
Inviting us to laugh and play,
In each crystal, stories gleam,
Awakening the deepest dream.

Nightfall Serenade

Softly the shadows stretch and sigh,
As daylight bids a sweet goodbye,
With every star, a note in tune,
The nightfall serenades the moon.

A gentle breeze whispers low,
Carrying secrets we long to know,
Crickets sing their evening song,
While the night wraps us along.

Darkness brings a soothing balm,
Embracing the world in a calm,
Every whisper of the trees,
In the night, our spirits seize.

Beneath the veil of twilight's glow,
Wonders await for hearts that know,
In this moment, we are free,
With the stars, a symphony.

Let dreams lead us through the night,
Guided by the soft starlight,
In this serenade we find our way,
Till the dawn breaks the spell we sway.

Moonlit Reverie

Under the moon's gentle embrace,
We wander in this sacred space,
Silver beams dance on the ground,
In their light, beauty is found.

Whispers of night call to the soul,
Enticing dreams to take their role,
In the stillness, hearts ignite,
Caught in the warmth of the night.

Memories twinkle like stars above,
Wrapped in the comfort of love,
Every heartbeat syncs with the time,
A melody, soft and sublime.

In shadows deep, our spirits glide,
As the moon becomes our guide,
In this reverie, we find grace,
Lost in the moon's sweet embrace.

Dreams unfold like petals in bloom,
Filling the night with ethereal tune,
As we dance in a world so grand,
Together forever, hand in hand.

Whispering Skies Above

The clouds drift softly, a gentle sigh,
Painting dreams on the azure high.
Stars awaken in twilight's glow,
Whispers of mysteries start to flow.

The moon hangs low, a silver thread,
Guiding lost souls where they are led.
Breezes carry tales of old,
Secrets woven, truths unfold.

As dusk embraces the world anew,
Fireflies dance in a shimmering hue.
Each flicker a story waiting to soar,
A reminder of what we long for.

Soft echoes linger, both near and far,
In the stillness where memories are.
Hearts bound together through time and space,
Lost in the night's tender embrace.

The whisper of skies above us shines,
In the silence, the universe aligns.
Dreams take flight, unbound and free,
In the arms of eternity we shall be.

Cosmic Harmony in Silence

Beneath the vastness of starry seas,
Harmony flows on the midnight breeze.
Galaxies swirl in a celestial dance,
A rhythm of life in a cosmic trance.

Nebulas cradle the light of dreams,
Whispers of space in luminescent beams.
Through voids and shadows, the echoes call,
A symphony woven for one and all.

In tranquility, the planets spin,
Boundless stories hidden within.
Each heartbeat a note in the vast expanse,
In silence, we join this grand romance.

Solar winds carry the tales to ignite,
In the fabric of cosmos, stars burn bright.
Every twinkle a promise made,
In the harmony of silence, fears shall fade.

Together we stand, at the edge of night,
Embracing the whispers of ancient light.
In cosmic harmony, our souls unite,
A dance of existence, ever so bright.

Frosty Vestiges of Day

Morning breaks over frosted ground,
Whispers of winter gently abound.
Crystals glisten in pale sunlight,
The world awakes from its frozen night.

Mist hovers low, a soft embrace,
Nature dressed in delicate lace.
Brittle leaves crunch underfoot,
In this stillness, life takes root.

Shadows stretch in the waking dawn,
Frosty remnants quietly withdrawn.
The chill in the air, a breath of grace,
Echoes linger in this sacred space.

Birds take flight on fragile wings,
Singing sweetly as daylight clings.
The sun ascends, a golden ray,
Warming the frost of yesterday.

Embers of night fade into the gray,
As the frosty vestiges melt away.
In every heartbeat, life finds a way,
Renewal whispers in the light of day.

Wistful Glows and Gales

The evening paints the sky in hues,
Wistful glows in vibrant blues.
Gales dance through the swaying trees,
A melody carried on the breeze.

Faded memories in shadows linger,
Soft whispers brushed by a gentle finger.
Nightflowers bloom as the stars align,
Their fragrance sweet, their glow divine.

In gentle swirls of the twilight air,
Time unfurls the stories it wears.
Every breath a wistful sigh,
As twilight bids the day goodbye.

The world slows down, tucked in embrace,
In the soft cocoon of twilight's grace.
Glimmers of hope in the fading light,
A promise of peace through the coming night.

Each gust carries dreams once spoken,
As daylight fades, and bonds are woven.
In wistful glows, we find our way,
Guided by the whispers of nature's sway.

Silence of the Midnight Sky

Stars whisper softly, lost in dreams,
The moon hangs low, casting silver beams.
Time stands still in this tranquil embrace,
A shimmer of peace in this vast, dark space.

Clouds drift slowly, like thoughts in flight,
Painting the canvas of this quiet night.
Each breath a secret, shared with the air,
In the stillness, we find solace rare.

Voices of shadows blend with the dark,
Crickets serenade, their song a spark.
The world outside fades, a distant sigh,
Wrapped in the silence of the midnight sky.

Hope floats gently on the wings of stars,
Each twinkle a promise, despite the scars.
We hold our dreams in the cool, crisp night,
In the silence, our souls take flight.

Embracing the calm, we let worries go,
Finding our heartbeats in the moon's soft glow.
This moment we cherish, forever will stay,
In the silence of night, guiding our way.

Glimmering Dusk

As the sun dips low, colors ignite,
The sky is a canvas, a breathtaking sight.
Brush strokes of orange, pink, and gold,
A story of day into night unfolds.

Birds take their leave, singing their song,
Nature whispers softly, all night long.
The horizon glows, a magical scene,
In the hush of dusk, everything's serene.

Trees silhouette against the glow,
A dance of shadows begins to flow.
The cool breeze carries secrets untold,
Wrapped in the warmth, as night takes hold.

Stars peek shyly, one by one,
The day's bright laughter is almost done.
We pause to breathe, to savor this time,
In the glimmering dusk, all feels sublime.

With every heartbeat, the evening calms,
Nature's embrace, a soothing balm.
In the twilight's grip, our worries fade,
In this sacred hour, memories are made.

The Frosted Horizon

Morning breaks softly, a world transformed,
Coated in white, nature's beauty warmed.
Frosted trees shimmer, a crystalline sight,
A canvas of wonder, pure and bright.

With each gentle step, the crunching sound,
Echoes of winter, all around.
The air is crisp, biting and clear,
Whispers of magic drift ever near.

Streams are silenced, frozen in grace,
Time stands still in this wintry space.
Bright sunbeams dance, casting playful light,
Across the horizon, a dazzling sight.

Winter's embrace wraps us in cheer,
A season of peace, drawing us near.
With hearts aglow, we cherish the day,
In the frosted horizon, worries drift away.

Moments are fleeting, like snowflakes that fall,
Each one unique, yet cherished by all.
In this fleeting winter, let love remain,
A bond that endures through sunshine and rain.

Echoes of a Winter Night

Under the blanket of a starry vast,
Whispers of winter come hauntingly fast.
The air is crisp, a knowing chill,
As shadows stretch across the hill.

The moon is a lantern, shining so bright,
Guiding lost souls through the quiet night.
Each rustle of leaves, each footstep soft,
In the echoes of winter, we drift aloft.

Footprints lead on, where secrets lie,
In the snow, a memory, as time flies by.
We gather around, sharing stories old,
In the warmth of the fire, our dreams unfold.

The night wraps us tight in its silken thread,
With thoughts of the future and all that's said.
In the gentle, still moments, we find our way,
In echoes of winter, we dream and sway.

Waking to dawn, a soft, golden hue,
Winter's embrace whispers tender and true.
Through the frost and the chill, our hearts ignite,
In the magic and love of a winter night.

Nightfall's Gentle Embrace

The sun has slipped beneath the hills,
Casting shadows, the night fulfills.
Soft whispers weave through twilight air,
A tranquil hush that beckons care.

Stars awaken, twinkling bright,
Guiding hearts through the peaceful night.
Moonlight dances on the trees,
A sweet serenade carried by the breeze.

Dreams take flight on silken wings,
As the world in sleep softly sings.
Night's embrace, a soothing balm,
Wrapping all in a mystic calm.

Glimmers of hope in darkened skies,
Reflecting fears and whispered sighs.
Under starlit canopies, we rest,
In Nightfall's arms, we feel our best.

So let the night be our retreat,
Where hearts converge and souls will meet.
In gentle stillness, we find escape,
In love's embrace, our spirits shape.

Wandering Lights of the Evening

Flickering flames in distant lands,
Guiding travelers with gentle hands.
Each light a story yet to unfold,
Whispers of dreams, both new and old.

The horizon blushes with fading day,
Crickets sing as they begin to play.
The skies, a canvas of deepening hue,
Paint a portrait of night imbued.

A dance of shadows across the ground,
As whispers of secrets begin to surround.
These wandering lights, a beacon of peace,
In their glow, all troubles cease.

Moonlit paths beckon the brave,
Where hearts find solace, and spirits wave.
A tapestry woven from night's embrace,
In wandering lights, we find our place.

So journey forth beneath the stars,
No matter near or far from scars.
In every glimmer, a chance to see,
The beauty in all that's meant to be.

A Chill in the Celestial Air

Cool breezes whisper through the trees,
Carrying tales of distant seas.
A chill in the air, refreshing and bright,
Wraps the world in a cloak of night.

Stars twinkle high, a luminous choir,
Filling our hearts with quiet desire.
The moon, a guardian in silver shroud,
Watches over as night is bowed.

In this stillness, time slips away,
As shadows dance in the softest sway.
Night's cool breath brushes the skin,
Awakens wonders that live within.

Under this vast, celestial dome,
We find our solace, a place called home.
Each chill breeze brings forth a new thought,
In icy caress, we seek what is sought.

So embrace the night, let worries cease,
In its cool grasp, discover peace.
For in the chill of the evening's air,
Lies a magic inexplicably rare.

Infinite Sparkle of the Night

A vast expanse, a sea of light,
Endless wonders grace the night.
Every twinkle tells a tale,
Of distant worlds beyond the pale.

Galaxies swirl in cosmic dance,
Captivating our souls at a glance.
Planets hum their silent song,
In the darkness where dreams belong.

Falling stars with wishes to lend,
Each fleeting moment, a precious friend.
In infinite sparkle, hopes take flight,
In the embrace of the starry night.

Constellations weave a tapestry bright,
Guiding the lost through the black of night.
A compass of dreams, so wondrous and free,
In this dark world, we find unity.

So gaze at the sky and feel inspired,
Breathe in the dreams that never tire.
In the infinite sparkle, all hearts ignite,
Together we soar through the magical night.

Radiant Frost

A crystal blanket glistens bright,
Soft whispers dance in morning light.
Each breath a cloud, a fleeting sight,
The world aglow, in hush of white.

Nature's lace on every tree,
Glistening gems, a sight to see.
Footsteps muffled, wild and free,
In this realm, where bliss shall be.

Frozen whispers, secrets told,
In silver hues, the dawn unfolds.
A symphony of bracing cold,
Embraced by winter's tender hold.

The sun ascends, it warms the air,
Yet frost still lingers everywhere.
A fleeting moment, oh so rare,
In radiant frosts, we find our care.

In twilight's glow, the frost retreats,
But memories linger and repeat.
Nature's artwork, soft and sweet,
A frosty dance, a graceful feat.

Ethereal Glow

A twilight canvas, painted skies,
Amidst the stars, where magic lies.
Ghostly whispers, softest sighs,
In every heart, the dreamer flies.

Veils of mist, a shimmered dance,
Caught in twilight's fleeting chance.
Every glance, a stolen glance,
In ethereal glow, we find romance.

Moonbeams twinkle on the lake,
Reflections stir, the stillness break.
The world transformed by night's awake,
In luminescence, hearts shall quake.

Soft as feathers, light as air,
In shadows deep, we shed our care.
With every pulse, a secret dare,
In this glow, we find what's rare.

As dawn approaches, colors blend,
A promise whispered, love will mend.
In every moment, we suspend,
In ethereal glow, our spirits ascend.

Twilight Embrace

Daylight fades, the shadows grow,
Beneath the sky, a softened glow.
Stars emerge, in twilight's flow,
A gentle touch, the world in slow.

Whispers of night, where dreams reside,
In twilight's arms, we safely bide.
Underneath the moonlit tide,
With every heartbeat, love won't hide.

Colors blur, the edges fade,
In this haven, worries laid.
A tranquil peace, a serenade,
Through twilight's veil, our fears betrayed.

The universe in stillness hums,
As night descends, the daylight succumbs.
In every night, the heart still drums,
In twilight embrace, the spirit becomes.

Each star a wish, each breath a dream,
Silhouettes dance, soft as a beam.
Together here, we find the theme,
In twilight embrace, forever we gleam.

The Silence of Stars

In the night's quiet, whispers reign,
The cosmos sings, a sweet refrain.
Stars align, a celestial chain,
In silence vast, love's sweet domain.

Each twinkle holds a story deep,
In shadows where ancient secrets sleep.
The heavens stretch, a canvas steep,
In the silence of stars, our dreams we keep.

Galaxies swirl, a dance divine,
In cosmic arms, our souls entwine.
Whispers of light, a gentle sign,
In the silence of stars, we brightly shine.

Lost in the depth of midnight's embrace,
The universe reveals its grace.
In starlit skies, we find our place,
In the silence of stars, we trace.

Together we gaze at the night's array,
Where every heartbeat finds its way.
In the silence profound, emotions sway,
The silence of stars, our hearts will stay.

Crystalline Nightfall

Stars flicker like distant flames,
Whispers of night, soft and tame.
A moon draped in silver light,
Guiding dreams through the velvet night.

Cool breezes dance on unseen wings,
Embracing the hush that twilight brings.
Every shadow a secret kept,
As the world around quietly wept.

Crystals shimmer on frosted ground,
Nature's beauty, profound, unbound.
In the stillness, hearts find peace,
As worries and troubles gently cease.

Night wraps the earth in an embrace,
Inviting the stars to take their place.
Each breath carried through the air,
A moment of magic, wonderfully rare.

In crystalline nightfall, we find,
The quiet lull of a wandering mind.
Under the cloak of the endless sky,
We whisper our hopes and let them fly.

Threads of Cosmic Air

Woven in whispers of ancient light,
Galaxies twirl in a cosmic flight.
A tapestry of stars, bright and rare,
Stitching together, threads of air.

Nebulas swirl in vibrant hues,
Painting the heavens with timeless views.
Each shimmer a story of loss and gain,
In the silence where wonders reign.

Comets trailing their frozen tails,
Course through the void as history pales.
Echoes of time gently draw near,
Threads of existence, both fragile and clear.

Starlit paths weaves dreams anew,
Guidance from skies, vast and blue.
In every inhalation, a stardust flare,
As we wander through threads of cosmic air.

From the depths of the universe, we rise,
Chasing reflections in infinite skies.
In the embrace of this celestial dance,
We find our place, a fleeting chance.

Enchanted Numbness

In the quiet glow of a fading day,
A spell is cast, where worries sway.
Soft murmurs cradle the restless mind,
In enchanted numbness, solace we find.

Dreams linger like shadows at dusk,
Wrapped in the magic of soft husk.
Every heartbeat whispers a tune,
Guiding the lost toward the moon.

Time drips slowly, a melting clock,
The world outside becomes a mere mock.
Wrapped in silence, we touch the divine,
In the haze of twilight, our souls entwine.

Moments extend, stretching like strings,
As we embrace what stillness brings.
In this cocoon of gentle embrace,
We lose ourselves in the vastness of space.

Enchanted numbness, a veil so sweet,
An escape from life's relentless beat.
In the whisper of twilight's caress,
We find our truths, we find our rest.

Glacial Gleam

Ice crystals forming under the moon,
Reflecting light in a winter's tune.
A glacial gleam, sharp and bright,
Carving silence in the deep of night.

Frost fingers touch the slumbering trees,
While whispers ride on the chilly breeze.
Nature's artwork, a stunning display,
As the world holds its breath, in stillness and sway.

Each flake dances with delicate grace,
In this frozen realm, time finds its place.
The night paints tales of wonder and awe,
In glacial gleam, where hearts withdraw.

Beneath the stars, a world so serene,
Captures the essence of all that's unseen.
With every glance, a promise shines,
In this glacial moment, our spirit aligns.

Whispers of winter, a tranquil hymn,
In frozen clarity, our days grow dim.
As the gleam fades into breaking dawn,
We carry its magic, ever drawn.

Nocturnal Reverie

Under the stars, whispers float,
Dreams entwine in shadows deep.
Softly sighs the nightingale,
In this realm where secrets sleep.

Moonlight bathes the silent trees,
Echoes of a time long past.
In the calm, the world feels close,
Moments stretch, forever cast.

Thoughts take flight on silver wings,
Wandering through the velvet dark.
In the stillness, silence sings,
Filling hearts with quiet spark.

Each heartbeat tunes to nature's song,
As shadows dance in soft embrace.
Here in dreams where we belong,
The night becomes a sacred space.

Awake in spirit, lost in thought,
A tapestry of dreams unfolds.
Night's embrace, a gift well sought,
In this realm where time is bold.

Moonlit Reflections

Beneath the glow of silver light,
Ripples weave on waters clear.
Memories shimmer in the night,
Guided by the moon's soft cheer.

Stars awaken, twinkling bright,
Casting dreams on azure seas.
Thoughts adrift in tranquil flight,
Carried gently by the breeze.

Echoes of a night well spent,
Whispered tales of joy and woe.
In the hush, the heart's content,
Found within the moon's soft glow.

Fragments of a fleeting hour,
Held in twilight's sweet caress.
Evening brings a gentle power,
A haunting peace, a softlessness.

In this light, intentions stir,
Bringing dreams to life anew.
With each pulse, a quiet purr,
Moonlit paths lead me to you.

Shimmering Solitude

Alone beneath the starlit sky,
Whispers of the night unfold.
The world fades, leaving a sigh,
In solitude, my heart feels bold.

Crickets sing their soft refrain,
Nature's chorus fills the air.
In their song, I find no pain,
Just a peace beyond compare.

Each flicker lights the darkened space,
Guiding dreams that start to bloom.
In this stillness, I find grace,
As the night consumes the gloom.

Echoes dance in gentle waves,
Rippling through the quiet night.
In the calm, my spirit saves,
A flicker of eternal light.

Wrap me in this sweet embrace,
Where thoughts and silence intertwine.
In solitude, I find my place,
A tranquil heart, a soul divine.

Chilled Essence of Twilight

Branches sway in evening's hold,
As daylight's blush begins to fade.
Whispers brush the earth, so cold,
In soft shadows, dreams are laid.

Hues of amber melt to blue,
Stars awaken, one by one.
In the hush, the world feels new,
Anticipation for what's begun.

Chilled air wraps around my skin,
A fleeting hint of night's embrace.
In this moment, deep within,
Twilight whispers softly, grace.

Time suspended, caught between,
The day and night, a whispered sigh.
In the dimming, stories glean,
Lives entwined beneath the sky.

As shadows stretch and twinkling starts,
Magic threads the dusk anew.
In the silence, beating hearts,
Find the night to push on through.

The Quiet Constellation

In velvet skies, the stars align,
Whispers of time in silent shine.
Dreams unfold in cosmic dance,
A tranquil heart finds sweet romance.

Galaxies spin, a tale untold,
Secrets of love in starlight bold.
Each twinkle holds a world so vast,
Moments suspended, forever cast.

Night embraces, a soothing balm,
Wrapped in wonder, pure and calm.
A constellation's silent grace,
Guides the wanderers to their place.

Through the void, hopes softly glide,
Each shining point, a gentle guide.
In the quiet, a soft refrain,
Eternal beauty we can't contain.

A universe of dreams conveyed,
In the dark, our fears allayed.
The quiet constellation gleams,
Filling the soul with silver dreams.

Shivering Echoes

Whispers linger in the air,
Shivering echoes, a haunting stare.
Footsteps fade on frost-kissed ground,
In the silence, lost dreams are found.

Moonlight glimmers on the trees,
A gentle rustle in the breeze.
Shivers dance beneath the night,
Echoes wrap the world in fright.

Memories stir in shadowed light,
Phantoms wander, taking flight.
Each heartbeat echoes, soft and low,
A chilling tale in the afterglow.

Beneath the stars, a lonely sigh,
Voices linger as they fly.
Shivering whispers, secrets keep,
In the stillness, shadows creep.

Yet hope remains in whispered dreams,
Among the echoes, light redeems.
Shivering echoes softly play,
In the night, they'll find their way.

Echoes of the Night

In the heart of night, shadows blend,
Fleeting whispers, dreams suspend.
Echoes linger, soft and clear,
Bringing distant voices near.

Stars above, a watchful eye,
Hushed supplications to the sky.
Echoes rise with every breath,
Life and love dance close to death.

The moon reflects a silver gleam,
Every shadow holds a dream.
In the silence, time slows down,
Echoes swirl, a ghostly crown.

With every moment, stories weave,
Tales of hearts that dare to believe.
In the depth of night's embrace,
Echoes find their destined place.

Secrets shared in tender light,
With every sigh, they take flight.
Echoes of the night resound,
In the darkness, hope is found.

Crystal Nightfall

As daylight fades to twilight's hue,
A crystal vision comes into view.
Twinkling lights on velvet black,
Whispers of magic fill the track.

Stars like diamonds, finely placed,
In the stillness, dreams are traced.
Nightfall's beauty, pure and bright,
Cradles the world in soft twilight.

Silvery mists begin to rise,
Framing secrets in the skies.
Crystal nightfall, a wondrous sight,
Wrapping the earth in soft delight.

Gentle shadows come to play,
In the quiet, hopes survey.
A canopy of splendid grace,
As dreams and wishes interlace.

With every heartbeat, time stands still,
In this moment, hearts can fill.
Crystal nightfall speaks so low,
In its embrace, we learn to glow.

A Winter's Lullaby

Snowflakes dance in gentle light,
Whispers soft as day turns night.
Blankets wrapped, the world sleeps tight,
Dreams take flight in silver white.

Moonbeams spill on frozen streams,
Nature's hush holds softest dreams.
Crisp and clear, the silence gleams,
Winter sings in peaceful themes.

Frosted trees in still repose,
Nights are long where cold wind blows.
Stars like diamonds, bright and close,
Time moves slow as nature flows.

In this quiet, hearts find peace,
Warmth and love begin to increase.
With each breath, the worries cease,
In winter's lull, life's joys release.

So let the night bring calm and cheer,
As dreams unfurl, we hold them dear.
In winter's lap, we draw near,
Awaiting spring, the time to cheer.

Glimmering Shadows

In the twilight, shadows play,
Glimmers dance at close of day.
Stars emerge in soft display,
Night unveils a grand ballet.

Whispers float on evening breeze,
Moonlight drapes the swaying trees.
Crickets chirp with graceful ease,
Nature sings in harmonies.

Glistening paths of silver hue,
The world transforms with each view.
Dreams emerge, both old and new,
In darkness, life's colors brew.

Mystic tales in silence creep,
Lost in thought, we drift, we leap.
Into realms where secrets keep,
In the night, our spirits sweep.

So let us dwell where shadows twine,
In the dance, our hearts align.
For in night's arms, we entwine,
Glimmering dreams and stars that shine.

Veil of Night

The sun dips low, the shadows blend,
Night descends, the day must end.
Stars ignite, the heavens send,
Mysteries on which we depend.

Darkness wraps the world in peace,
In the stillness, fears release.
Fading echoes, moments cease,
In silence, find a sweet increase.

Veils of night conceal the day,
Hidden paths where dreams can play.
Each whisper holds a soft ballet,
In twilight's hush, we drift away.

Moonlight bathes the earth so bright,
Guiding souls through the soft night.
With each heartbeat, shadows bite,
Yet in their clutch, there's pure delight.

So let the dusk embrace our minds,
Within the dark, the magic binds.
In night's embrace, love intertwines,
Veil of night, where hope unwinds.

Astral Caress

In the cosmos, we find our place,
Stars above in a tender embrace.
Celestial dance, a timeless grace,
Each twinkle holds a hopeful trace.

Galaxies whisper, secrets unfold,
Stories of dreams in stardust told.
In every glimmer, visions bold,
Hearts ignite in the vast and cold.

Beyond the sky, where wishes soar,
Infinite wonders forever explore.
In cosmic tides, we long for more,
An astral kiss upon the shore.

Across the night, our spirits ascend,
Each heartbeat echoes, time will bend.
In the light, with love, we blend,
As stars align, our souls transcend.

So let us chase the heavenly light,
In the vast expanse, we reunite.
Together, we embrace the night,
In the cosmos' arms, we'll take flight.

Frosted Tapestries on the Boughs

Delicate lace upon the trees,
Whispering tales with the breeze.
Crystal gems in morning light,
Nature's charm, a wondrous sight.

Glistening drops that slowly fall,
Nature's artwork, enchanting all.
Branches bow with silent grace,
Frosted beauty, a soft embrace.

Winter's breath, a subtle kiss,
Moments like this, we can't miss.
Beneath the weight of frosted veils,
Magic stirs as silence prevails.

Each twig dressed in icy lace,
Time stands still in this sacred place.
The world transformed, so pure, so bright,
A tapestry of purest white.

In this realm of frozen dreams,
Life pauses, or so it seems.
A quiet hush, a tranquil hour,
Frosted tales of winter's power.

Enigma of Winter's Gaze

In shadows deep the silence lingers,
Patterns formed by frozen fingers.
Misty veils that dance and play,
Whispers of night, hiding the day.

Footprints mark the blanket white,
Stories shared beneath the night.
Crystals sparkle in moon's embrace,
Each breath a ghost in this vast space.

A riddle wrapped in winter's shroud,
Where dreams and echoes weave a crowd.
Frosted dreams in each cold sigh,
Questioning where the answers lie.

Stars retreat in cloak of snow,
While shadows twist and gently flow.
Underneath this chilling air,
Lie secrets waiting to ensnare.

In the stillness, hearts align,
Finding warmth where paths intertwine.
An enigma cloaked in night,
Winter's gaze, a gentle light.

Glinting Wonders in the Void

A canvas dark, so vast, so wide,
Contains beholden truths inside.
Each twinkle speaks in silent tone,
Mysteries of the unknown.

Galaxies swirl with endless grace,
Lost in time, we find our place.
Moments fleeting, yet so clear,
Glimmers shine and draw us near.

In the stillness of the night,
Dreams take flight, seeking light.
Glinting wonders, stars that weave,
Stories of those who dared believe.

Across the sky, the dappled hues,
Kiss the lips of midnight blues.
Cosmic dances, fleeting flights,
Life unfolds in starry sights.

In that void, we find our call,
Infinite beauty that enshrouds all.
Entwined in the dark, we explore,
Finding light forevermore.

Beneath the Harsh Luminance

Where shadows blend with blushing dawn,
Harsh lights flicker as hopes are drawn.
Life's harsh edge lays bare the truth,
In every crease, a lingering youth.

Beneath the glare, hearts beat slow,
Underneath the weight of woe.
Lost fragments of forgotten days,
Resurfacing in waning rays.

Bright illusions dance their dance,
Yet in their glow, we find our chance.
Moments captured, fleeting fire,
From harsh light, we find desire.

Endless journeys, roads untold,
Stories of the brave and bold.
Beneath the harshest light we stand,
Finding strength in mystery's hand.

Though the glare may blind our gaze,
Within the fire, we learn to blaze.
Every shadow, every shine,
Teaches us how to entwine.

Frostbound Illumination

In the hush of winter's breath,
Stars shimmer on the frost,
Moonlight spills like silver threads,
Whispers of the night embossed.

Each flake dances in the light,
Crafting glints on barren trees,
Crystal dreams in coldest sight,
A serene, enchanted freeze.

Night unfolds its velvet cloak,
Painting shadows, deep and wide,
Silent stories softly spoke,
As dawn begins to bide.

Beneath the sky, a world asleep,
Where secrets rest on icy ground,
Yet in this calm, the heart can leap,
In stillness, hope is found.

Frostbound stillness, whispers clear,
A moment caught, ethereal,
In the chill, it draws us near,
To the magic, undeniable.

Enigmatic Nightfall

Veils of dusk descend so shy,
Stars awaken, flickering bright,
Mysteries loom as shadows sigh,
The world transformed in fading light.

Cloaked in secrets, whispers low,
Each heartbeat echoes in the dark,
Glimmers dance like a shadowed show,
Enigma draped in twilight's spark.

Branches sway with softened grace,
The moon ascends, a ghostly guide,
Barely seen, yet fills the space,
Night's embrace both fierce and wide.

In the hush, a story weaves,
A tapestry of dreams untold,
Every heart the night deceives,
In its depth, the brave and bold.

As stars collide in cosmic play,
The night invites the lost to roam,
In this realm where shadows sway,
The magic of the night feels home.

Dreaming in the Milky Way

Underneath the starlit skies,
Galaxies swirl in endless flight,
Every wish a spark that flies,
Whispers of the cosmos bright.

In this ocean of the void,
Dreams unfold, both vast and free,
Celestial paths, a light enjoyed,
Infinity holds the key.

Nebulas bloom in splendid hues,
Travelers drift on cosmic streams,
Stardust glows in midnight blues,
Woven softly into dreams.

Each heartbeat syncs with cosmic sound,
While comets arc through velvet night,
Among the stars, new worlds are found,
In this dance of endless light.

Dreaming there in vast array,
Amongst the jewels of the sky,
Navigating the Milky Way,
Where heart and universe comply.